Love
Letters
from Parents to Teens

Love Letters
from Parents to Teens

MARLENE RIDDLE

ARCHWAY
PUBLISHING

Archway Publishing books may be ordered
through booksellers or by contacting:

Archway Publishing
1663 Liberty Drive
Bloomington, IN 47403
www.archwaypublishing.com
1 (888) 242-5904

Because of the dynamic nature of the Internet, any web addresses or
links contained in this book may have changed since publication and
may no longer be valid. The views expressed in this work are solely those
of the author and do not necessarily reflect the views of the publisher,
and the publisher hereby disclaims any responsibility for them.

Any people depicted in stock imagery provided by Thinkstock are
models, and such images are being used for illustrative purposes only.
Certain stock imagery © Thinkstock.

ISBN: 978-1-4808-1528-5 (sc)
ISBN: 978-1-4808-1529-2 (e)

Library of Congress Control Number: 2015901860

Print information available on the last page.

Archway Publishing rev. date: 2/18/2015

With love I dedicate this book to my grandchildren
Drew and Alexis (front cover), Calan, Karissa,
and Faith, who have showered me with
infinite joy since the day they were born!

 *Introduction*

There is a formidable chasm in the world of adolescents today which needs to be filled with the highest level of principles and directions. Parents need to be assembled in their goals, holding each other's hands, and establishing the most effective ways to meet their needs. Their entire future will depend on the spiritual food they are being fed by their parents and educators, during these very short years they will be under your wings – nineteen years, as compared to the fifty-plus years they will likely be on their own. Give them the best you can. Be available at all times, as they are treading perilous grounds, full of traps and temptations.

Many parents assume that they can finally relax, as their children approach adolescence. They cannot be farther from the truth! This is a crucial mistake. This is when your teen will need you the most. In their tender years, they were enjoying a safe nest, protected by the wings of caring parents. Now they are getting strength, looking around, assessing the terrain, uncertain whether their wings will sustain them in their first flight attempts. Brand new situations will present themselves, intriguing, frightening. Your offspring will look around for you, trying to remember all the lessons you taught them during their young years. There are many voices uttered by their peers. They are powerful, coming from everywhere. Which ones should they heed? Which ones will lead them to a happy, fulfilled future?

Dear parents, statistics show that 51% of teens are afraid of talking to their parents about personal, private problems. It is even slightly higher - 54% - when it comes to talking to their teachers. (Stageoflife, Teen Trend Report: "Teens and Fear," 2013)

What are parents to do? One solution would be to encourage them to write you about these problems. If you take the first step, writing to them, they may like the idea, finding it less threatening, and will start writing back to you. With time, these letters will no longer be necessary, and you and your teens will be talking to each other person to person, having great conversations, all in an atmosphere of trust and harmony.

This book gives you some examples of letters

written by parents to their teens. My other book, "Love Letters from Teens to Parents", will give your adolescents ideas on how to approach you with their personal problems in written form. Welcome such letters, discussing them with kindness and understanding. Give them your full attention.

My best wishes for this new undertaking! If you like to write, and if you feel inclined to contact me, sharing your experiences and giving me suggestions on how I can improve my future writings, you may reach me at:

MARLENE RIDDLE
riddlema@verizon.net

 *Trust Me!*

Dear _____,

How many times I feel inclined and inspired to put my arms around you, look at you serenely, calmly, and invite you to open your heart to me! I know there are so many things you want to reveal, discuss with me, but you do not know how I would react. Don't be afraid, my child! I want to be the best friend you have ever had in your life.

You can trust me with your most intimate feelings, assured that they won't be revealed to anyone, if you so desire.

There is a very special reason I was chosen to be your parent, and I thank God every day for this blessing! I also ask Him to help me be deserving of this choice. I want to be there for you always, without causing too much pressure but giving you the space you need to grow and become strong!

Come to me anytime you need an attentive ear and a heart to confide in. If you are concerned about something you did that is not giving you peace of mind, or feel that you need to tell someone in order to relieve your mind, count on me! I cannot say that I will approve of what you did every time, but I won't condemn you either. Feeling bad and uneasy is already part of your punishment, and feeling sorry is already part of your salvation. Learn a lesson from it, and decide not to let this happen again. Ask God's forgiveness and I will also pray for you to stay strong in your decision.

Much love,

_____

Walking With You Side By Side

Dear _____,

When I look at you, I remember when I found out you were going to be part of my life and my world! What joy! How many dreams! Then, when I held you in my arms for the first time and our eyes met, my mind sent you messages of everything I was feeling! There were so many things I wanted to understand and absorb.

I prayed for God to make me worthy of such an important mission: to be a kind, patient, devoted, available, forgiving parent!

Today, I still want to be to you the kind of parent I desired on those first days! Tell me, dear: How am I doing? Am I fulfilling my deepest desires? Am I being there for you anytime you need a person in whom to trust and confide? Am I being an attentive listener? Am I giving you the time and space you need to grow, to blossom? Am I trustworthy and determined to make your life an amazing experience?

I want you to know how proud I am of everything you have already accomplished in your life and how wisely you have learned from your failures and disappointments. I want to walk with you side by side, supporting you in your dreams, forgiving your mistakes, helping you make the right decisions, and praying for you to have a very happy, fulfilled adolescence!

Love,

_____

Life Is All About Relationships

Dearest _____,

I waited for the arrival of your teenage years with great anxiety! Many parents fear and avoid thinking about these brief seven years of their children's life, but not me! Knowing you as I do, I am totally confident that you have been well prepared to face and enjoy this transition time.

There is a false connotation associated with the word "teenager" that frightens many adolescents. They become confused, not knowing what to expect. Relax, my child! There is nothing that we, together, cannot overcome. There is a solution to every problem, and together we will find the best answer to every challenge.

Remember, life is all about people, relationships. If you learn to treat everyone well, with kindness, respect, forgiveness, even if your fellow high schoolers do not reciprocate, you will be able to overcome all obstacles and guarantee a happy adolescence!

Count on me every time you want to share your feelings and thoughts. The journey will become easier and smoother this way. If we disagree about any aspect of your experience as a teenager, explain your beliefs and points of view to me. It is very possible that we will find many ideas and common ground between us!

Much love,

_____

 *Choosing Your Friends*

Dear_____,

Do you know that the years between thirteen and nineteen are known as the wonder years?

However, many people don't agree. They say this is the most difficult time of their lives. Why are you assuming that, if you can cross the bridge that leads you to a more mature stage of your life, everything will be okay? Not so! You need to make the most of your wonder years; otherwise, your adult life might become a rough sea of confusion, regrets, and loneliness.

How can you make the most of your adolescence? Can this stage be the most wonderful time of your life? Have you ever heard or read about a "happy, successful teenager"?

What are the ingredients for a smooth, exciting teenage life? Does this depend solely on having a nice house, great parents, money, a great body, brains, and talent? Wouldn't this be extremely unfair? Consider movie stars, famous athletes, rich kids. Are they always the happiest ones? Are they always the most balanced, content, grateful, and pleasant adolescents? Sometimes, it is just the opposite! How many do we know who have had a deplorable ending?

Talking to teenagers, we find that, first of all, the happy ones are those who are content with what life has offered them, which is not always the ideal situation. They try to make the most with what is available to them. They are usually fairly good students, responsible, smart when choosing their friends and those they will hang out with. They are not influenced by the "popular group" but make their own decisions. They are pleasant and fun, treat everyone with respect, help those in need. They are hardly ever bored or depressed.

We, your parents, did not come to these conclusions easily. We had to learn the hard way, through many disappointments and much pain. Now we share them with you, as you are the most important human being in our lives, and there is nobody else we wish the very best life can offer!

Much love,

_____

Marlene Riddle

How to Deal With Bullies

Dear_____,

Sometimes, you come home from school very bro-kenhearted, saying that a student called you a hurtful name. Teens love to attach labels to their peers, saying with disgraceful words that they are too tall or too short, too fat or too thin, too brainy or too dumb, too rich or too poor. They say terrible things if a person's nose or ears have unusual shapes or sizes; if the person belongs to a different race or nationality, if the person has an accent, if the person dresses a little peculiarly. Some of these bullies happen to have uncommon characteristics themselves, but they be-lieve that if they label others first, this might prevent others from labeling them, thus granting them some immunity.

What should your reaction be if bullies call you names? Absolutely nothing! Ignore them, even if they call you "chicken" or "coward," when you do not react. Move away, without looking at the offender. If you are with a friend or friends, continue your conversation, while distancing from the troublemaker. If the situation worsens or continues on the following days, however, report it to a teacher, counselor, or principal. We, as parents, should also be informed. Leave the consequences in our hands!

Much love,

_____

 *Jealousy*

Dearest_____,

You confided to me today that Ben, your boy-friend, is extremely jealous and does not even allow you to talk to other boys. He is very hot-tempered and, sometimes, you fear he might hurt you. Let me tell you what happened to my best friend, Liz, when we were in high school.

She was dating a very handsome, cool, popular guy. He was very thoughtful and considerate but excessively jealous. One day, he saw her walking and having a conversation with a teen from one of her classes. Without even asking for an explanation, he immediately broke up with her. She was devastated, as they had been dating for almost a year. Then she realized that, if the relationship progressed and they got married someday, she would never have been happy, as his jealousy would have ruined their marriage.

She started dating other guys and finally found one who was well-balanced and had enough self-esteem to maintain a pleasant, trusting relationship. Many girls become desperate when their dating does not work well, thinking it is the end of the world. Not many dates work well and lead to marriage. If this occurs, great! If not, try to date different guys, with different personalities, but with the same principles as you have.

With love,

_____

 *Labels*

Dear _____,

You told me the other day that your good friend, Morgan, was thinking about changing schools. I would advise her not to. The girls treat her badly because they are very jealous. She is pretty, gets good grades, is a cheer leader, and is a talented ballet dancer. So they want to give her a hard time.

I spoke to her mother a few weeks ago, and she said that Morgan even cries in the morning, begging to miss school, as she can't take it anymore! She does not care about moving to another school, even if it is not as well recognized academically as the one she is attending now.

I advised Morgan's mother to speak to the school counselor or principal and report what had been happening. I said, "They will take some action, I am sure." You, as a good friend, need to make sure to stand by her side at all times, teaching her to peacefully hold her ground and not let anyone despise her! Morgan is a kind, gentle, peaceful girl and does not deserve to suffer bad treatment from her schoolmates!

Much love,

_____

Marlene Riddle

# The Popular Group

Dear _____,

Today, when I asked you why you have been so depressed lately, you replied that there are a few students in school who do not seem to like you or appreciate your efforts to be kind to them. I completely understand how you feel. You are not the only one in this situation. It is impossible for us to please everybody, it does not matter how hard we try! Some students waste an entire school year striving to impress and be accepted by some popular groups, without success. A smart school counselor suggests, "Try once, try twice, and if you are not accepted or appreciated, give up and go find fish in another pond. They do not deserve you!"

Do you remember Brooke, a neighbor we had when we lived in California? It was very important for her to belong to the popular group, even though their values and goals in life were so different! You advised her to leave the group and make friends with some girls who were more compatible with her beliefs, even if they were not so popular. Brooke resisted the idea, reluctant to leave the "in" group.

In the middle of the school year, Gilda, a smart, attractive, fun girl moved to your school, and Brooke soon introduced her to the popular group, sure that she would be accepted. That was not the case. The group became very jealous of her, so Brooke had a very important decision to make: choose between Gilda and the popular group. She chose the former. In the following weeks, Gilda became your best friend.

When prom time came, the girls of the popular group had a terrible fight. Graduation became a nightmare, a time of hurt feelings and disappointment for all of them. I was so happy and proud that you and Gilda made better choices and were able to end the year with flying colors!

Much love,

_____

Bullies and Low Self-Esteem

Dear _____,

I read in the newspaper that a bully annoyed a student to such an extent that this teen felt he could not take it anymore. So, he started giving the provoker a terrible time, humiliating him in front of other students, destroying his school materials, and laughing at him. The result was that both ended up in the principal's office, the parents were called for a meeting, and the teens ended up being suspended.

My children, bullies act like this out of fear and insecurity, although this is hard for us to believe. They are usually unhappy, with low self-esteem. They believe that being the attacker will prevent them from being the target.

If you are the victim of bullying, treat the offender in a Christian way, avoiding retaliation. Hold your ground, but in a peaceful way. They, as everybody, deserve respect and consideration, even if you are not treated the same. If this approach does not work, and the problem continues, talk to us, your parents, and we will take the case to the school counselor or the principal.

Much love,

_____

Marlene Riddle

 *Don't Suffer in Silence*

Dear _____,

I was grateful to you last night when you decided to open up to me and share the reason why you have not been as cheerful and joyful as usual lately. I have asked you for the reason a few times, but you were not willing to reveal what was causing your depression. Youngsters usually prefer to suffer in silence than to reveal what they think will worry or upset their parents. I can understand that.

Remember, my child, that when you are in low spirits, your parents should be the ones for you to seek. We are the ones who love and know you the best. We will give you all our time and attention, as soon as you request it. Don't fear that we will be mad or yell at you. You and I will sit down calmly and discuss the problem, just like we did last night. I will be "all ears".

Parents want to be an integral part of their children's life, and when they trust us with their troubles and difficulties, we feel extremely happy to help.

Affectionately,

_____

Marlene Riddle

Make Your Own Decisions — Sometimes

Dear _____,

You seem surprised when, sometimes, I let you make your own decisions. The reason is that I want you to grow up, to mature. We are not giving up our responsibilities as parents. When we decide to allow you to make certain decisions, we do so after careful consideration. Each case is brand new, is another experience to explore, and our decision is made according to your age and social development. It is crucial that we do not overestimate your capacity to discern what is right and wrong at this particular stage of your life. If we misjudge the right time for you to make certain decisions, consequences may turn out to be very unfortunate, sometimes leaving scars that will last a lifetime!

Much love,

_____

 *A Smooth School Life*

Dear _____,

I have interviewed many teens who have just finished high school, asking what they thought was one of the most important factors in assuring a smooth, pleasant school life; what they would do differently if they had to go through high school all over again.

Many of them replied, "Hanging out with the right crowd." When asked "Why?" they explained that having two or three mature friends, who used common sense and knew how to make smart choices, not caring about being popular or in the "in" group, would keep them on the right track and away from dangerous, wild experiences!

I am interested to know your opinion! Tell me which high school experiences have made you mature so far. Have you had the opportunity to learn from poor choices?

With love,

_____

# Leave the Consequences to Me

Dear _____,

Parents are told to love their children unconditionally, just like God loves us. You have been going through tough times lately, and my heart suffers also. Many children don't understand that, when they are going through difficult times, many parents are also suffering inside, sometimes a hundred times more! So, my dear one, let's embark in this healing process together.

I heard something today that really made me think. The words were, "If your children really love and trust in you, they will do the things you teach them." I think this is so important because, when youngsters get out of their parents' counsel, that's when they get into trouble. After counseling, parents should say, "Do this, and leave the consequences to me." Be strong and of good courage! Better times are ahead. This, too, shall pass!!

Much love,

_____

 *Enjoy Your Adolescence!*

Dear _____,

Enjoy your adolescence as much as you can! You will be an adult for many more years than you will be a teen. Being in your stage of life is a privilege!

Act with responsibility, but don't try to act as an adult. Enjoy your age! Be proud of it! Be a role model as a teenager, the best teen possible! Experience the joys of your younger years!

There will be many years in your life when you will be required to act as a reliable adult. That is when you will be seriously tested. If you are a responsible teen now, it is very likely that you will become an adult who is dependable, trustworthy, righteous, with great character and integrity!

Love always,

_____

We All Just Want to Be Loved

Dear _____,

When your birthday arrives, I wish I could offer you many gifts, the things I know you like the most. All parents feel the same way, but many cannot afford such luxury. You have been very understanding and grateful for everything you receive. I appreciate it so much!

A 15-year-old boy wrote, "When it comes down to it, what we all want is to be loved." The unhappiest teens are the ones who lack affection and feel lonely. They carry with them a feeling of emptiness and have no purpose in life. Teenagers like people who appreciate and approve of them.

Every seventy-eight seconds a teenager ends his life in the U.S. Billy Graham, the famous evangelist, said that the main reasons for suicide among teenagers are: lack of affection, fear of failure, loneliness, and emptiness. I believe that "lack of affection" supplants all!

Two million American teenagers live on the streets, lonely, confused, with no affection!

You told me once that we, parents, bless teens with our presence, not with gifts; that these are secondary, coming "in addition to our time and attention." Yes, my children, you need our love, our encouragement, our praise for every small victory you achieve!

Much love,

———————————————

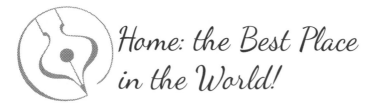# Home: the Best Place in the World!

Dear _____,

Now that you are growing up, I am delighted to see that we are all striving to reach the same goal: to live in an atmosphere of love, peacefulness, harmony, kindness, consideration for one another. This has been happening naturally at our home because we all desire, most of all, that our home be the best place in the world to live!

All of you make an effort to solve your problems and differences in a sensible way. You cannot imagine how grateful and fortunate we, your parents, feel.

What I remember the most about my life, when growing up, was how happy we were when spending time together at home. My parents always spoke in a calm, pleasant voice, so the kids grew up learning to follow their example.

We hope that this will be an important legacy we are leaving you. May you always remember how happy our home was and follow the same guidelines when you start building a family of your own!

    Much love,

_____

Rod of Discipline or a Gentle Spirit

Dear _____,

What would you prefer: that I came to you with a rod of discipline, or that I came in love and with a gentle spirit?

My parents never hit us; we were grounded instead. We accepted the consequences. My parents tried to make us understand the reason for such a decision. All parents also had some difficult times as teens, made mistakes, suffered the results, and learned their lessons. Now, with their own teens, they try to spare us as much pain as possible, also because of love. Teens think that they are going through difficult times, that adults don't understand them, but they forget that being the parent of a teenager is quite a challenge!

We want our kids to succeed more than anything! Our greatest goal is to deliver to society young adults with great character and family values, responsible, strong in spirit, kind, considerate, and hardworking.

Remember how much we love and are proud of you! Raising you has been an invitation to victory! With much affection,

_____

 *Encouragement*

Dear _____,

I am writing not to condemn or criticize your way of living, but to encourage and comfort you. When I say "encourage" I mean to approve your effort to follow where your conscience and principles are leading you.

You are being led by an extraordinary power, the Lord Jesus, pulling you away from discouragement and confusion. Allow this power to take hold of the oars, making you surrender to a life of honor, beauty, purpose, and grand design! Wipe away the fog from your eyes and delight in the vision that unfolds before you!

Love always,

_____

 *Vision and Purpose*

Dear _____,

In a few years, your high school program will be over. I know that you have been thinking, for quite a while, about your college years, making plans for a successful four-year program! You are aware that this is the time when you will continue being molded to perform in society. Whose shoes are you going to wear? What will be your role in this world? What is your vision and purpose for your life?

It does not matter what your college plans are we, your parents, want you to remember that we desire to continue being part of your life, just as it has been for the past eighteen years! Share with us your interesting experiences, as well as your difficult moments. Come and visit us anytime! We will be delighted to have you!

Much love,

_____

No More Loneliness

Dear daughter,

When you started high school, you got home depressed and unhappy sometimes because you didn't have any friends. I sympathized with you and tried to give you encouragement. I used to say, "It is better to be lonely for a while, and happy with yourself, than to belong to a group of popular students and feel miserable."

It did not take long before you started talking to Dinah, a smart, sweet, attractive girl, whose family had just moved to the US. Her father was a diplomat, and they immediately treated you with great kindness!

You now have not only Dinah as a friend, but a small group of cheerful, fun, responsible girls. I am so glad that you made the right decision, seeking friendship among youngsters of great character!

Much love,

_____

 *Choose Your Dates Wisely*

Dear _____,

One of my best friends told me an experience she had had in her life. When she was in college, her grandfather, whom she loved very dearly, told her that she would make him extremely happy if she married Geoffrey, son of her mother's best friend. They had gone to many dances and parties together; he was a perfect gentleman, very handsome, with the same principles and goals as she had, and a brilliant future ahead. He had already asked my friend to be his steady date, but she replied that she was not ready to make a serious commitment yet.

The problem was that she had no romantic feelings for him. Her parents and friends all agreed that they were the perfect couple. She told them that she would never marry a man with whom she was not completely in love.

Many young adults feel pressured to marry somebody based on his or her social status, looks, family notoriety, financial situation, all of which take priority over their feelings and principles. Dear children, don't ever allow such factors to take precedence over what really matters, if you are looking forward to a happy and lasting marriage!

Much love,

_____

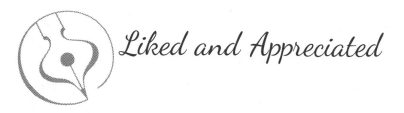 *Liked and Appreciated*

Dear _____,

When I read about a youngster who was chosen "the most likely to succeed in life," or "the most congenial" (pleasant, agreeable) person in a group, I made a mental list of the qualities I believed such person would have. I thought about prom kings and queens, who many times are not the best-looking students in high school. What would their secret be? Why would their colleagues vote for them? Could it be their positive outlook on life, their awesome personality, their unpretentiousness and modesty, or the kind way they treated everybody?

It is important for us to be liked. It makes us more content with life. It makes us more prepared to face the trials we all have to face sooner or later.

People who are liked are enthusiastic, optimistic, fun, friendly; they smile a lot; they don't talk about themselves all the time, but are interested in other people's life and interests; they don't criticize others; they help those who are having problems or going through a difficult time in their life; they are not proud, but admit when they are wrong; they are courteous, polite; they don't hurt people's feelings or embarrass them in front of their peers; they are kind and pleasant.

So, what do you think? Could you add to this list? Could you be included in this group with at least fifty per cent of such qualities?

One thing is for sure: most of us improve with age, with the lessons we learn, some of which are very painful. However, parents love their teens without restrictions, supporting them at all times, encouraging them, and cheering for every victory they attain! This includes their social skills and the refinement of their spiritual traits!

Love always,

_____

Vision Impaired and in Charge

Dear _____,

I watched an interesting real story on TV last night about a nineteen-year old youngster who was extremely successful at golf. His father had trained him since a very young age. However, when he finished high school, his vision started failing him, and it got worse with time.

His parents took him to consult famous specialists, without success. He became legally blind and could not play golf anymore. He thought his life was over, and became extremely depressed.

Today, he is 24 years old and told a TV interviewer that he is happier today than he was in high school. He found an organization that trains golf players with vision impairment, even promoting competitions. He is now a motivational speaker, and is invited to many schools to encourage visually impaired boys and girls to become in charge of their lives. They are encouraged to follow their dreams and explore all their possibilities, just like Helen Keller used to do.

I just wanted to share this with you because nobody knows what awaits us in the future; but, whatever happens, we should be prepared to make the most out of it. We, as parents, wish the best for our children, but also want them to have the character and strength to overcome with grace and dignity all the obstacles that life places in their path!

With love,

_____

Prepared for the Unexpected

Dear son,

I was completely shocked when I heard on the radio this morning, on my way to work, that a 16-year-old boy had driven while intoxicated the night before, killing four other people.

Things like this can dramatically and suddenly happen when we least expect, changing our life forever. This kind of news opens our eyes, alerts us, changes our ways. Can teens continue to live the same lifestyle after learning about such tragedy? Some believe that they are immune, and that this will never happen to them.

I want to compliment you, my son, for your good judgment, discernment, and soberness. Continue being a role model to teens. Stay away from friends who entice you to do what might bring tragic consequences, ruining your future forever.

Affectionately,

_____

 *Peer Pressure*

Dear children,

You ask us sometimes if we had peer pressure during our teenage years. You think that being an adolescent was much easier in our days.

You are right to a certain point. Maybe we didn't have such a strong peer pressure because we didn't have social media. For example, a 13-year-old girl recently jumped from a tall building because she had been bullied for a long time through YouTube. Students had been sending her messages such as, "You are not worth anything", "You are very ugly," "Nobody likes you," "Why don't you kill yourself?" and so on.

My children, I don't want you to ever believe defamatory, depreciating things you read about yourselves on any social media. They are not true! Those kids have no character, no courage to say those things face to face.

If this ever happens to you, make sure you share it

with us, so we can take the necessary steps to immediately stop such harassment!

Love,

_____

Marlene Riddle

# Dropping Out: Statistics

Dear _____,

How many of your classmates have you witnessed dropping out of high school? It is so sad that parents don't enforce the completion of such an important investment. If the students don't want to attend college, it is also sad, but at least they will have a better opportunity in life than those who quit high school. Parents should have complete control of their children's education until at least they reach eighteen. Sometimes, especially among low-income and single-parent homes, they are asked to leave school early in order to join the work force and contribute to the family's income. There are 1.2 million students dropping out of high school every year, in the United States alone! When they get married and start a family, almost half of them are on welfare. Also, of all the convicts in prison, 65% are dropouts!

If you have students in your class who are planning to drop out, talk to them about these statistics and encourage them to not give up! They desperately need counsel and sound advice. Be a friend! Contribute to this nation's educational excellence! We were number one in the world in this area forty years ago, as opposed to nineteenth this year. You can make a difference, my child!

Much love,

_____

 *Trust Can Be Regained*

Dear _____,

 The best gift you can give us, your parents, is our trust in you. You have done great so far, and we are very proud of the way you have conducted yourself as a teenager! Not many teen parents can say the same. They lose trust in their children when they fail to tell them the truth. One episode only is enough for the parents to lose confidence in their youngsters, and then it might take weeks, or even months, for that trust to be restored, even when teens repent and apologize. It is so sad! Parents will always end up forgiving them and loving them just the same, but the experience is sometimes painful.

 Much love,

_____

Consideration — Always!

Dear _____,

Remember when we were riding our bikes around the lake this morning? It was a beautiful sunny day and there were many people trying to enjoy the warm weather, after weeks of cold and rain. The children's playground was crowded, and there were no parking spaces available nearby.

I noticed that a new, expensive car had been parked in the middle of two parking spaces, to make sure nobody parked next to it. Drivers passed by, looking for a space, and when they saw the two spaces being occupied by just one car, shook their heads, in disapproval.

That was not the first time I had seen such selfishness. Those are public parking spaces, and everybody has the same right to occupy them. If people want more room, they should park elsewhere, even if it is a paid space and not so close to the desired area!

My children, always respect the rights of other

citizens and try to help everybody you can. Walk the extra mile. Offer your services. Most of all, assist the elderly, the handicapped, the mother with little children, the poor. Be a model teen, and you will be richly blessed!

Much love,

_____

 *I Was Born to Succeed*

Dear_____,

Unfortunately, my father passed away when I was a teen. He had always been my best friend.

Our house was not big, and he didn't have an office, so he placed his desk in the family room. The desk had a thick glass on top, and he used to place cards with famous sayings under it. Every time my sister and I walked by, we casually glanced at the cards and, little by little, started memorizing some of them. I had two favorites: "I am absolutely sure that I was born to be a success in my life" and "The best recipe for happiness is to be kind and helpful to others."

It is hard for us to understand how sayings like these, when repeated regularly, make an impact in our life. Negative sayings are just as powerful. I wish the authors of TV commercials and composers of songs for the youth used this principle to influence the life of our youngsters for the better! Instead, they

infiltrate and poison their minds and their lives unin-
terruptedly, little by little!

Affectionately,

_____

# T.W.A.: Thought, Word, Action

Dear children,

Did you know that everything you do in your life starts in the form of a thought? You decide if you want to "dismiss" this thought, or "entertain" it. You are the decision maker. If the thought does not make you comfortable, you have the power to change it immediately into something constructive, positive, worthwhile, before it starts creating power.

From the mind, thoughts change into words. You talk about them, or write about them. Negative or positive, your thought is now becoming more powerful; it is creating a life of its own. However, you still have control over it: you can change or modify it while there is still time.

Next, the thought is transformed into action. We act upon it. I like to call the entire process "TWA": thought, words, action. For example: a bully in your class makes fun of you and embarrasses you in front of the other students. A thought (T) comes to your mind: revenge! You are going to trip the troublemaker as he leaves the room, after class, and everybody will laugh. It is a bad thought, so you have the chance to remove it from your mind while you can. Maybe a better idea would be to confront the instigator after school and ask him why he had embarrassed you in front of the other students (A), for no reason at all. You are going to tell him that it had been a bad idea, explain to him how you felt, that you expect this never to happen again, or there will be consequences. If the youngster has any regrets, this will be a great opportunity for him to apologize. In this case, you can have an intelligent, mature discussion with the offender.

My children, think carefully before reacting harshly in critical times, if you want to avoid regrettable and dangerous consequences!

Much love,

_____

Empathize: it Will Make You Proud of Yourself

Dear daughter,

I cannot express how proud I was when you invited our neighbor Priscilla to your birthday party! Due to her physical disability, she is not invited very often. The other youngsters believe she won't feel very comfortable for not being able to join in all the games and activities, so they prefer not to invite her rather than to hurt her feelings. You, however, took the risk, decided to give her as much attention as possible! You mean a lot to her!

Priscilla's mother is a devoted lady, doing everything she can to provide her daughter with as many opportunities as the other teens have. Priscilla is also a sweet and kind youngster.

During the entire party, I watched closely how caring and attentive you were to Priscilla, making sure she blended well with the other guests. She seemed comfortable and relaxed, having fun watching the activities, even when she could not participate in them.

Priscilla's mother said that, after that party, the other teens started relating better and more spontaneously to her daughter, thus improving her self-esteem and social skills.

Thanks again, daughter! I couldn't be any happier and more grateful for your sweet, great heart!

Much love,

_____

 *Mother's Day*

Dear _____,

Thank you for all the attention you gave me on Mother's Day! I was very emotional when I read your card! You deserve everything your dad and I do for you! You have always honored and respected us, filling our life with joy!

When you say "I love you," you not only say it with words, but prove it with actions. I know that sometimes you don't agree with us, do not support our decisions; still, you try to understand our point of view, being respectful and considerate. This shows your character and means so much to us, your parents!

Thanks so much for representing our family so well in school, church, and our community in general!

With much love,

_____

Your Friends Are Important to Us

Dear_____,

Feel free to bring home some of your friends, once in a while, to complete your homework together, finish a project, do research, or simply to visit! I want to have the opportunity to know them, talk to them, see what they have to say. Friendships are extremely important, at this time of your life! I don't want to compare you with them, or expect them to be your carbon copy. I respect your individuality. I would never say, "I don't want you to bring your friend here ever again!", or "You are prohibited to hang out with this kind of friend!"

I trust your ability to select your friends. Of course, they will have personality, dreams, interests different from yours, but when it comes to character, a decision has to be made!

You won't want for a friend a youngster who lies, steals, uses improper language, has bad manners, and is not loyal to you, as a friend.

You are probably thinking that I am too "picky" or "choosy" about everything in your life. You might be right, but are you familiar with the commercial "There is so much riding on my tires?" That's how I feel about my responsibility as a parent! You are a precious "cargo" in my life, and I have the divine duty to take you through this wonderful journey safely and cautiously!

Much love,

_____

What I Like the Most About You

Dear_____,

Do you know what I like the most about you, teenagers? Your enthusiasm! Even when you go through hardships, you keep your excitement, passion, zeal, fascination for life!

What helps is that most parents remember that their youngsters need constant encouragement. They encounter setbacks but bounce back fast, reinvigorated, full of energy and zest!

My children, let no one despise your teenage years! Nobody has the right to spoil, ruin, damage these short, important seven years of your life!

Affectionately,

_____

 *Take a Chance: Be Nice*

Dear son,

You told me the other day that one of your friends commented that everyone took advantage of you because you were "too nice!" You asked me, a little hesitantly, if it was a good or bad thing to be "too nice".

What is important, son, is to know what it means to be "too nice". At the same time that you show kindness to everyone, you must also establish the limits of how the others should treat you. They should show you the same respect, consideration, politeness, regard, civility that you show them. When you are kind and courteous to others, they should treat you the same way. If they don't, you should let them know that they are "crossing the line"– not with an argument or angry words, but with dignity and self-control. Your serious expression will tell them everything! Never reply with offensive, harsh words. This would give them a chance to continue disrespecting you. Some people say, "Hold your ground."

Yes, we should do this, but in the correct sense of these words.

Good luck, son! You are on the right path!

Love,

_____

Marlene Riddle

 *Your First Job*

Dear child,

You just got your first job. Congratulations! You deserved it. You tried so hard to do everything right: arrive at the interview on time, wear clean and appropriate clothes, be courteous and respectful to the interviewer. How exciting!

I am also very happy to know that you realize that this job will likely be on your records in all of your future jobs. It will be like a "letter of recommendation," telling your future employers how well you did in this first experience.

How can you build a good reputation, so it will be easier to find better jobs, with better pay, in the future? How can you "beat the competition" against more experienced candidates? How can you guarantee that you won't be fired, thus marring your employment record from the beginning?

First and foremost, don't miss work, unless you are very sick or in an emergency situation. Good attendance is essential, vital, imperative. Many managers or business owners, when having to choose between an employee who has excellent attendance and another with more experience, but is absent frequently, will choose the former one.

Be perfectly clean. Shower daily, have your nails trimmed and clean, hair combed, clothes clean and appropriate, without having to be expensive. Girls, keep your makeup simple and your clothes decent, proper.

Be honest. Don't remove from your work money or materials owned by the company, it doesn't matter how small or inexpensive they are. This is extremely important, and if reported on your records, it will be very difficult for you to get a new job.

Treat your boss, co-workers, and customers with respect and courtesy. Do your job the best way you know, trying to improve from day to day.

Well, good luck, my child! I am confident that you will do well, and that this will be an exciting experience for you. Anytime you want to share or discuss anything about your work, make sure to count on us.

Much love,

# You Are Important and Valuable

Dear daughter, son,

One thing that is very important for teenagers is to have self-confidence. Never let other people – brothers, sisters, friends, teachers, and even us, your parents – make you doubt how valuable and important you are.

You told me, when you were in elementary school, that your teacher taught the students to let negative comments about them "go in one ear and out the other". One boy told the teacher, with tears in his eyes, that his father had said that "he would never amount to anything". His best friend immediately went to the chalkboard, got an eraser, handed it to his friend and said, forcefully, "Erase that thought, right away!" His teacher couldn't help but smile.

Children, make sure you feel confident that your appearance, talents, personality, character, beliefs, values, are of the finest quality. The same way, never make anybody feel humiliated, embarrassed, put down. Some negative comments may stay with a person for a lifetime, hurting their chances for a successful life!

With love,

_____

Marlene Riddle

 *Stick to the Truth*

Dear _____,

    Since you were very young, maybe age four or five, your father and I started teaching you how to always tell the truth. Lies corrupt and are very damaging! At first we only had a nice conversation, explaining how important this was in our family. There was no serious punishment, as we didn't want you to be afraid of us. As you grew older, however, when this happened, we felt we should enforce our teaching by deciding on some consequences. These were generally being grounded or deprived of some privileges. You learned your lesson, not wanting us to lose our trust in you.

    It is such a joy to have children who are faithful to the truth! I praise you for your effort and determination to make your words as valuable as gold!

    Lovingly,

_____

Demonstration of Affection

Dear _____,

I read today about a teenage boy who was planning to end his life the next morning because his father had never told him that he loved him. Some parents are very reserved and don't display their feelings very openly, but this does not mean that they don't love their children very dearly!

It happened that, the day before, some workers at the company where his father worked received a trophy, in recognition for their outstanding performance at work. The man thought and thought, and then decided to give the trophy to his son. That night, after dinner, when he gave the trophy to his son, the told him that he loved him very much, and that he deserved the recognition even more than him, as the teen was a great student, and always received excellent grades.

The boy sobbed and sobbed, and finally told his father what his plan was for the next morning. Now, his plan had no longer a reason for being, as he knew his father really loved him. Children should never think that their parents don't love them, if they don't say it or demonstrate it very often. Children are the most important people in their parents' life!

Love,

_____

Marlene Riddle

 *Parties: Which Ones to Attend*

Dear _____,

You were quite excited last weekend when Joseph invited you to a party at his house. You thought you knew him well, as you have been in the same school for a couple of years. You also knew well the students who had been invited, so you were very relaxed and certain that everybody was going to have a great time.

That evening, you came home early and totally disappointed. When we asked what had happened, you explained that, to your surprise, the teens were consuming alcoholic beverages, using drugs, smoking cigarettes! Joseph's parents were not home, and young couples were isolating themselves in different rooms of the house.

You felt devastated, as you thought Joseph had the same principles as you. He should have let you know ahead of time what kind of party he was planning to give, so you could make a decision whether or not to attend. Besides your determination of not getting involved in such situation, your presence there would indicate that you approved of what was happening, that you were "one of them". Your name would be connected to a group of youngsters who were not "your kind of crowd." I know, however, that this was not your main concern. To you, what matters the most is to preserve your good character and the name of your family!

In such a difficult situation, you made the right decision: you said goodbye to the host, thanked him for the invitation, and left almost unnoticed. No complaints, no criticisms, no comments. You were not there to judge.

Love,

_____

Marlene Riddle

Matters That Need Your Attention Now

Dear children,

Some teens are very reserved and quiet regarding particular issues, expecting and even hoping that their parents take the initiative of approaching them with questions. It happens that parents don't always know if their teens prefer to be left alone for the meantime, and deal with certain matters at a later date, or if they should initiate a conversation as soon as possible. Most parents are well aware that certain matters should not be left alone!

Children, let us know, without delay, if there are issues where you need to have answers right away! Don't trust just any source. It's nice to have friends in whom to confide, but many times they don't have enough experience and maturity. Trust us, your parents! Don't be afraid of being grounded, lectured, or criticized, as this won't happen. All we want is to be your best friend and make sure you trust in us unconditionally!

Much love,

_____

Marlene Riddle

# The Way You Dress

Dear daughter,

Many teen girls have such low self-esteem that they believe the only way they can get attention from the guys is wearing provocative, seductive clothes, and heavy makeup. What a mistake! Yes, many boys are attracted to this kind of girl, but not with good intentions. They are not the ones you would like to have as a serious boyfriend, or even as a date. They just want to enjoy the "benefits" they can get from this kind of relationship. The next thing they do is to boast to a group of friends what the two of them did, and how far he was allowed to go. The next few days, when the girl walks through the school halls, she hears laughs, whispers, and hurtful comments.

My daughter, when girls dress like that, they are placing on themselves a "price tag," and the guys will know how much they are worth.

The more provocatively they present themselves,

the lower the price on the tag. It is the same as if they were saying, "I am up for grabs. Help yourselves."

Dress with modesty, elegance, good taste!

If you want to wear makeup, do so in such a subtle way that it will enhance your natural, beautiful features!

With love,

_____

Conversation Versus Physical Confrontation

Dear children,

Since you were little kids, you have been taught not to fight, have heated arguments, or even physical confrontations. Every day, how many times kids are punished, grounded, yelled at, for their lack of self-control, be it at home, school, sports competitions, and the neighborhood in general?

This is not surprising because, when they turn on the TV or go to a theater, all they see is violent movies, wars, and disharmony. Politicians claim that we should solve our differences using diplomacy, and not bloody disputes. What is diplomacy? It is trying to solve our differences with other countries using harmony, fairness, agreement, tolerance, good sense, and not with fights and wars. Diplomacy is something that we could also use at home, work, or school through mature conversation, trying to reach agreement without using physical force.

There are about 134 wars going on in the world

today, only because the responsible parties decided not to use diplomacy. The same way, there are physical confrontations between teens just because they forget they can solve their differences just by having a sensible conversation. Animals fight because they cannot talk.

Children, don't let other teens convince you that, if you refuse to fight, you will be considered a wimp, a coward, or a "chicken". It is just the other way around! They are the ones who don't have the courage to resolve problems peacefully.

We, as parents, have the obligation to teach our children to have self-control, to become civilized individuals. Many of you will become important leaders someday, responsible for the peace and stability of your own country!

Love,

_____

Temptation

Dear _____,

   I had a conversation with a school counselor recently and she told me that many adolescents confess that it is very hard to resist temptation. She lovingly explains to them that one sure way to resist temptation is to <u>stay away</u> from people, places, and things that tempt them. She advises them to seek the company and friendship of teens who have been brought up never to get involved in any improper or destructive behavior. Christians learn that, "if they resist the devil, he will flee from them". Although the devil can tempt them, he can never <u>force</u> anybody to do anything they don't want to do!

   With love,

   _____

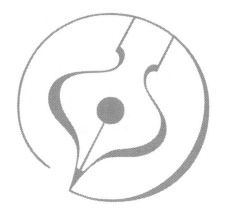

# We All Make Mistakes

Dear _____,

Thank you so much for opening up to me and trusting me with your problem! We all make mistakes. I understand. Let's talk again about what happened, so you will feel less troubled.

You failed one of your classes and regret it very deeply. The consequences at school will be serious. You didn't take this subject seriously enough, giving more importance to classes you enjoyed more. Your dad and I won't punish you more than what you are already being punished. We know, however, that you will learn from this lesson and will never let this happen again. You have been very responsible all year and deserve some credit. Continue counting on us in difficult times. We are the ones who love you the most!

Love always,

_____

Are My Parents Being Reasonable?

Dear _____,

    As parents, we are told not to exasperate our children. "Exasperate" means irritate, provoke, torment, pester, and harass. We are supposed to be calm and patient while teaching our children about life, to seek our Lord, to honor and obey their parents, so things will go well for them and they will enjoy a long, happy life.

    However, some teens think, "What if my parents are not being reasonable? What if they are demanding well beyond what we are able to accomplish?"

    Instead of disobeying, request to have a calm conversation with your parents. Try to reach an agreement or a compromise. When your parents prevail, then you will need to wait until you have your own children, so you can establish your own rules. Parents have more experience and wish their kids the very best!

    Trust them!

    Love,

_____

 *Consider Double-Dating*

Dear daughter,

You have been dating Ethan more frequently now, and I notice that the feelings you have for each other are becoming stronger. This is the time when youngsters make very important decisions. If they have high principles and strong convictions about how they should behave, they are going to feel somewhat confused, perplexed. Does the guy really value his girlfriend and want to do the right thing?

The best decision is for both of you to avoid being completely alone in isolated places, or in a situation where self-control would be very difficult. A good idea is for teenagers to double-date with youngsters who share the same beliefs. Many teen girls are worried about losing their boyfriend if they do not agree with his requests. Double-dating may relieve the stress of difficult situations.

Daughter, I feel that Ethan really cares and values you, and that you are both well prepared to make wise decisions about your relationship. Come to me whenever you have questions, or just want to have an intelligent, open conversation. Be confident! Everything is going to turn out fine!

With love,

_____

 *Career Choices*

Dear _____,

You told me the other day that you would like to be in the entertainment business when you finished college. Many parents want their children to be a carbon copy of themselves, following similar careers. I believe this is a great mistake, although the parents have the best of intentions. Children have different abilities, inclinations, personalities, and dreams. They come to this world with their own "suitcase," equipped with all the things they will need to fulfill their mission on this planet. If we, as parents, will guide them to use wisely all the abilities they brought with them when they were born, encouraging them and providing opportunities for their development, we will be raising accomplished individuals, potential leaders in their own field. Conversely, if the parents' only objective is to lead their children to careers where they can obtain riches and power, their youngsters will be unaccomplished and unfulfilled.

Children, we will respect your decision, while giving you some orientation and advice, as parents should do, but within your chosen field!

With love,

_____

 *Finding Fault*

Dear _____,

I have been thinking about what you told me a few days ago. You said that you like your English teacher this year more than the one you had last year. When I asked you the reason, your answer was very interesting. You said that when these teachers corrected your essays, your previous teacher wrote many comments, but all very negative, only criticizing. Conversely, this year's teacher wrote many compliments, accentuating the positive and downplaying the mistakes. She explained the errors with kind, encouraging words. The students considered her a friend, an ally, a cheerleader. Due to this approach, your grades in English have improved considerably!

My child, this makes me think that this is also what happens with our friendships. When we constantly find fault with every little mistake our friends make, we will soon lose them and become unpopular. Cherish your friends! They will bring joy without end to your life for many years to come!

Love always,

_____

Marlene Riddle

 *Laugh at Your Own Mistakes*

Dear _____,

Blessed are those with a healthy sense of humor!

Think about all the students you have had as classmates throughout the years. Which ones were the most liked: the ones who smiled the most, or the grumpy ones, who were always in a bad mood? Which ones had more friends?

A famous singer said that you will grow up when you learn to laugh at your own mistakes, and not at the mistakes of others. Many teens believe that what makes them liked and popular is to make fun of other teens, mostly in public. This is disgusting, and should not be accepted.

Teens who have a good sense of humor are also more optimistic, have more self-confidence, and enjoy life every day! They smile more, and don't let criticism affect them.

It has been said, "Champions face life with enthusiasm and refuse to be offended!"

Love, and more love,

_____